The Digamma

THE
SEAGULL
LIBRARY OF
FRENCH
LITERATURE

WORKS OF YVES BONNEFOY
AVAILABLE FROM SEAGULL BOOKS

The Arrière-pays
Translated by Stephen Romer

The Present Hour
Translated by Beverley Bie Brahic

The Anchor's Long Chain
Translated by Beverley Bie Brahic

Rue Traversière
Translated by Beverley Bie Brahic

Toegther Still
Translated by Hoyt Rogers

Ursa Major
Translated by Beverley Bie Brahic

Poetry and Photography
Translated by Chris Turner

Rome, 1630: The Horizon of the Early Baroque
Followed by Five Essays on Seventeenth-Century Art
Translated and edited with an afterword by Hoyt Rogers

The Red Scarf
Translated by Stephen Romer

The Digamma

YVES BONNEFOY

CENTENARY EDITION

Translated and with a Foreword by
HOYT ROGERS

LONDON NEW YORK CALCUTTA

A number of the English translations appeared previously in the literary journals *AGNI*, *Cerise Press* and the *New England Review*. I would like to thank all concerned for their kind cooperation.

Hoyt Rogers

www.bibliofrance.in

The work is published with the support of the
Publication Assistance Programmes of the Institut français

Seagull Books, 2023

First published in French as *Le digamma* by Yves Bonnefoy
© Éditions Galilée, 2012

First published in English translation by Seagull Books, 2014
English Translation © Hoyt Rogers, 2014

ISBN 978 1 8030 9 296 6

British Library Cataloguing-in-Publication Data
A catalogue record for this book is available from the British Library

Typeset by Seagull Books, Calcutta, India
Printed and bound by WordsWorth India, New Delhi, India

CONTENTS

FOREWORD
Hoyt Rogers   *vii*

God in *Hamlet*   1

Leaving the Garden, in the Snow   17

The Digamma   21

Learned Libraries   27

The Works of the Unconscious   30

Voice in the Sound of the Rain   33

More on the Invention of Drawing   38

For a Staging of *Othello*   40

The Great Voice   52

The Digamma: A Final Note   59

FOREWORD

Yves Bonnefoy is generally considered the finest translator in France as well as the greatest French poet, and he is particularly renowned for his numerous translations of Shakespeare. His fascination with the defining author of our language is amply reflected here in 'God in *Hamlet*' and 'For a Staging of *Othello*', two poems in prose that belong to an ongoing series of meditations on the plays. Though these are elaborate tributes, passing allusions to Shakespeare are frequent throughout Bonnefoy's work, and provide English speakers with a special access to his poetry. For example, we easily catch the unexpected echo of *Romeo and Juliet*—with all its overtones of impending disaster—in the final words of the title poem, 'The Digamma'. While the backdrop of most pieces in this collection will also seem familiar, several of them may call for a brief introduction.

Inveterate readers of Bonnefoy will recognize immediately that 'Leaving the Garden, in the Snow' fuses two themes that have come to the fore in the later phase of his life-work—the banishment of Adam and Eve from Paradise and the enigmatic message relayed by the snow. The biblical motif is linked to the author's lifelong interest in Italian art, expressed most often in his essays on aesthetics—for example, the book-length excursus *Rome 1630: The Horizon of the*

Early Baroque, published in 1970. But he does not fully develop the topos in his lyric production until 2008, in the prose poem 'Une variante de la sortie du jardin' (Leaving the Garden: A Variant), which harks back to a landscape painter of that era, Nicolas Poussin's son-in-law, Gaspard Dughet. In the same collection, *La longue chaîne de l'ancre* (The Long Chain of the Anchor), 'Une autre variante' (Another Variant) proposes a more searing vision of the expulsion from Eden, this time inspired by the fifteenth-century artist, Masaccio. Both these treatments had been adumbrated earlier by a light-hearted poem, 'Le peintre dont le nom est la neige' (The Painter Named Snow); wryly, it alludes to Adam and Eve in cold-weather togs, strolling through the snow. This new version of the legend from Genesis, 'Leaving the Garden, in the Snow', elaborates on that earlier vignette, while investing it with the weightier tone of the two longer 'Variants'. As in 'The Painter Named Snow', Bonnefoy identifies the snow with a unifying language that almost seems to heal a fallen world. Though it has reappeared fairly often since then, the motif dominates the 1991 collection *Beginning and End of the Snow*, sparked by the novel surroundings of a six-month stay in New England. In these and other works of the last two decades, snow becomes an emblem of the poet's words, swirling and ephemeral. A transitory whiteness seems to purify the earth; but redemption, like the weather, comes and goes. As Emily Dickinson describes its ambivalence, the snow 'traverses yet halts— / Disperses as it stays'.

Like 'Leaving the Garden, in the Snow', 'The Works of the Unconscious' joins two frequent themes of Bonnefoy's recent poetry—in this case, the persistence into the present of civilizations long extinct and the role of children in defining the lyric self. The former topos has been a constant in virtually all his books but in his current phase it has taken on an added dimension—rather than interrogating cultures that existed historically, as in his previous writings, he has begun to generate them out of his own sensibility. In 'The Works of the Unconscious', he goes one step further, and floods his extant books with pages from vanished languages, part of the submerged but lingering awareness we have accumulated over our many millennia on earth. Significantly, both the author of these nocturnal works and the single sentences within them are portrayed as children. Children range through Bonnefoy's texts of the past twenty years with gathering insistence, as though the poet were reliving his earliest youth. Archetypal but never abstract, they may often be understood as symbols of poetic clarity, the wide-eyed wonder of a simple gaze. But for that very reason, they are powerless to unravel the conundrum of what our unconscious mind may 'write', individually or collectively—whether in our dreams or in the 'dark backward and abysm of time'. The startled child at the end of 'The Great Voice', the poem that closes this small collection, affords another example of the same motif.

A key passage of the title piece of the book, 'The Digamma', may pose a quandary for many English speakers. It relies on an image that has been iconic for generations to every schoolchild in France, though less widely known in other countries. Poussin's *Shepherds of Arcadia* depicts three men and a statuesque woman in ancient dress, gathered before a mysterious tomb in the countryside. The tenth and eleventh paragraphs of 'The Digamma' detail the pastoral setting and the four figures with lively exactitude, as any educated French reader would instantly recognize. The painting was traditionally considered the epitome of French Classicism, a concept that has fallen out of favour. Nowadays, as in Bonnefoy's *Rome 1630*, the art of seventeenth-century France has taken its place in the greater context of the European baroque. Though Bonnefoy has written extensively about Poussin, he sets him apart as a solitary genius rather than as the representative of any broader style. In his magnificent analysis 'Les Bergers d'Arcadie' (The Shepherds of Arcadia), he identifies the canvas as crucial to the artist's evolution, and 'The Digamma' mirrors many aspects of that essay. The sustained reference to Poussin's iconography serves to ground the text in the lost civilizations of antiquity. Subtly, it brings out the underlying theme that finitude informs every facet of human life: as the tomb's inscription states, 'Et in Arcardia ego'—'I [am] even in Arcadia.' In this connection, Bonnefoy touches on the age-old debate about the tacit verb 'sum', which Latin grammarians find unnecessary to the semantics of the phrase.

The omitted predicate might imply that like the digamma, absence always functions as a presence; in the ambiguous world we inhabit, being and non-being are fundamentally one.

Hoyt Rogers
Santo Domingo–Forlì, 2013

WORKS CITED

BONNEFOY, Yves. *Beginning and End of the Snow* (Emily Grosholz trans.). Lanham, MD, and Plymouth: Bucknell University Press, 2012. Originally published as *Début et Fin de la neige.* Paris: Mercure de France, 1991.

——. *La longue chaîne de l'ancre* (The Long Chain of the Anchor). Paris: Mercure de France, 2008.

——. 'Leaving the Garden: A Variant', 'Another Variant', 'The Painter Named Snow' in *Second Simplicity: New Poetry and Prose, 1991–2011* (Hoyt Rogers ed. and trans.). New Haven, CT, and London: Yale University Press, 2012, pp. 226, 236, 170.

——. 'Les Bergers d'Arcadie' (The Shepherds of Arcadia) in *Dessin, couleur et lumière* (Drawing, Colour and Light). Paris: Mercure de France, 1995, pp. 117–48.

——. *Rome 1630: L'horizon du premier baroque* (Rome 1630: The Horizon of the Early Baroque). Paris: Flammarion, 1970.

GOD IN *HAMLET*

I

The rehearsals had begun fairly well. But right away, puzzling events started to take place. First of all, the director felt a restless, overpowering urge to expand the stage—the usual space wasn't enough for him any more. Already on the second day of our meetings, he wanted to knock down a wall left over from a former stage set and in his impatience he grabbed a hammer and banged at the painted boards. But they held firm; they wouldn't budge an inch. He had to give up, in a fit of tears.

We were amazed. But the desire to enlarge the scenic backdrop soon spread to the actors. They liked to keep their distances from each other. You might have said they wanted to leave the stage empty. The actor who played Polonius, a portly man with a slight limp, was always straying here and there, as if searching for cracks in an invisible wall. Perhaps those would provide him with the air he seemed to need. We kept having to call him back from wherever he was, and he only returned with regret. As for the young lady who had been chosen for Ophelia, somewhat by chance, she liked to sit off to one side, staring blankly ahead. One morning she let out a cry and jumped up, holding out her tremulous hands. Then it appeared that she wanted to flee, but where? She collapsed a few steps further on—like the director, racked by tears. Hysteria? Come now, not a bit—she was always so thoughtful, so calm.

Soon the director decided we had to leave the theatre behind; he led us far, far away into the bleak landscape of that country. In a field, under the vast, lowering sky of this remote corner of the world, the actors would shout when they moved away from each other—shout to make themselves heard in the scene then being studied. With delays, their voices would double back as echoes from the nearby cliff, making them mingle. At such times we came to love those harmonics, which clouded the sound and even the meaning of the words.

We would meet early in the morning on that expanse of grass riddled by sharp little stones; they were hard on Ophelia and Gertrude, who lurched along in their high heels. Polonius always arrived somewhat late, limping with things he carried from home. He insisted on showing them to us and even blending them into the action. He would place them here or there, sometimes hide them in a clump of brush. They were humble objects, since the actor was poor. One time he brought a long board, still bearing traces of reddish ochre. Another time it was a painted plate, with flowers and fruits closely intertwined. Two verses written on the plate in a naive hand said that 'the god of Cythera' loves 'mystery'. On a certain morning, when there was a storm, our Polonius showed up with a little girl—his daughter, who was patently furious. Though she resisted, he dragged her along. When he let go of her hand, she ran all the way to the big stone at the end of the field and sat there, sobbing.

II

I'll say nothing more about the other oddities of those first days. They amused us, they even disturbed us a bit; but they didn't make us uneasy, so we tried to forget them. Still, it was something else again when undefined spasms overwhelmed certain actors—to the point of choking them—who right before had been placidly endeavouring to master a scene. First it happened to Ophelia. We knew that Hamlet had entered her room a few days earlier, bearing all the marks of amorous frenzy—doublet undone, incoherent words, quaking hands. And she had been afraid. Wasn't he the heir to the throne, possessed of awe-inspiring power? And didn't she love him as well, without admitting it as yet to herself? Good reasons for being moved during this new encounter, especially since today the mad prince insulted her with astonishing words.

But the actress playing this part had given no indication that she was the least bit impressionable. I have called her detached, even standoffish. We now saw her follow the director's bidding with great care—he wanted her to portray a daughter who obeys her father without question, though he has set her an onerous task indeed. As we know, Polonius wishes to prove to the queen and king that her son, and his stepson, loves Ophelia. Her duty is to provoke Hamlet through her coyness into avowing his feelings for her once again. Meanwhile, the other three are concealed behind one of the tapestries that assume such a central role in the play. As for tapestries, we had none of those on this moor where puddles glistened after a recent rain. Claudius and Gertrude and Polonius simply keep quiet, a little to one side. And then the young prince appears—well, not so young any more—muttering something or other about life and death, being and nothingness. He breaks up with Ophelia—and yes, he insults her—even if he tells her he had loved her all the same. Then she must murmur, 'Indeed, my lord, you made me believe so.' After that Hamlet will reply, 'I loved you not'—though without convincing us. And Ophelia will say, 'I was the more deceived.'

She managed to say the first words, but when she came to the second line an immense flailing coursed through her body. Her throat stopped up, making her words unintelligi- . ble, and she was wrenched by sobs. Her arms flew up; they seemed to tear away from her, to float in space for an instant under the sky that had brightened again. Then she collapsed into the mud, prostrate and still trembling. She never looked at her companions, who fell over themselves to help her to her feet; she never even saw them. Was this a repetition of her bizarre outburst the other day? Merely the emotion of an actress, at the most climactic moment of a scene that was undoubtedly intense? No, her dazed eyes were rolling too wildly for that, when they managed to stand her up again, and her head was tossing back and forth. She had been assailed, but by what? By whom? The rehearsal had to be postponed—though could they ever take it up again?

After this there was a similar emotion, mysterious because excessive, which seized one of the actors—that is, the thespians Shakespeare included among the personae of his tragedy. It happened when he was declaiming a fragment from a work in his repertory: the story Aeneas recounts to Dido, already madly in love with him, about the final hours of Troy. Hamlet was listening raptly. The actor headed the troupe newly arrived at Elsinor, and perhaps the prince meant to propose that, on a later evening, they should present this play, or poem, which he recalled for its clarity as well as its aplomb. The strange thing was that he knew entire passages of it by heart, and he had begun reciting his favourite, the death of Priam—speaking the verses with a flair all his own, at least in the opinion of Polonius. Even so, he soon broke off and deferred to the professional actor.

We listened along with Polonius, and all was going as well as might be wished—the players struck just the right tone of nonchalance and amusement, lending this conversation between actors and theatre lovers the naturalness intended by Shakespeare. But when the actor caught up the words left hanging by the prince, he immediately struck me as struggling against an emotion that had pervaded him, a feeling that rapidly grew. He continued his declamation, yet allowed the foolish Polonius to interrupt him; then he took it up again and came to the death of Hecuba. By now his knees were wobbling and his voice sounded strangled. This time once more, the author of the play wanted emotion, and he himself was clearly moved. The evocation of Priam overcome by blows, and of Hecuba in her distress, is as gripping as we can imagine. Saying these verses, superb in themselves, is more than enough to make you change colour and to fill your eyes with tears.

But that scream! It was the howl of a mortally wounded animal—no, even worse. The actor bellowed it out, just as he was recalling the shriek Hecuba herself had flung at the face of the gods on the walls of Troy. That cry welled up from an abyss I cannot conceive within any human being. It engulfed the sob of the old woman, fused with it and shattered it—carried her shriek high into the sky, yet preserved it all the same. Undoubtedly, the shout of this tottering man was inherent to the text, but it was something far more—and something different as well, wholly different. It conveyed a terrible suffering but also gave proof of an extraordinary sweetness—if I may put it so boldly—in that hoarse, enormous voice. As with Ophelia several days before, I had the impression (we all had the impression) that a power beyond all measure had slipped into a being of slighter size and had ravaged it—though once again, more in order to identify itself with that lesser being than to destroy it. Besides, the actor soon recovered his spirits. He told us that he had seen, at the instant of his scream—had seen, simply seen—the face of Hecuba and her poor hands reaching towards Priam's bloody body. But just as he was saying that, people shouted behind us. Someone had noticed that the actor playing Hamlet had fainted; he lay a couple of paces away from our group, his forehead resting on tufts of grass.

We rather liked this man who played the title role; though his temperament was somewhat reserved, he was always affable and considerate. In this case, he stood up without a word and commenced his work with the director again as soon as he was needed. Even so, it was he who soon afforded us the greatest of our surprises. I will try to recount it but I know I will never succeed. This time it is night, and the drama devised by Hamlet, about a king murdered by his brother, has just been broken off. The actor portraying the prince must show the joy he has felt at the discomfiture of Claudius, who has also killed his brother. But on the emptied stage, Rosencrantz and Guildenstern now come forward—courtiers who are clearly spies. And Hamlet will mock them, will leave them confounded and abashed, in the well-known scene of the recorders. He has several of those instruments brought forth, and ironically bids Guildenstern to make music with them for him.

And so the actor who is Hamlet picks up one of the flutes; he holds it out and displays the holes the fingers need to cover. We watch him, the rest of us, as he prepares to grab a hand that pulls away and to guide it with a laugh—he had mastered that little laugh—towards the slender wooden pipe, lit by the three or four lamps the director had requested. But suddenly, our friend froze in place, as if struck by an unexpected thought.

He looked around him, right and left, in this night that enveloped us all. He looked at us—and with such uncanny eyes. He looked at the recorder—and immediately, he seemed to awaken. He pressed it to his lips and played it, though he had never done so before. And believe it or not, for some time a wondrous music poured forth, which I can only call divine. Like nimble shadows, his fingers danced along the glowing holes. Unbelievable sounds issued from this little object, normally employed for the teaching of birds. The world all around us—the darkness, the wind—stirred in its depths, as if it might disintegrate. This music from somewhere outside it filled those humble, earthly forms with its violent beauty, both too perfect and too simply human . . . Does what I am saying here make sense? I won't try to describe any further what was unsayable from the beginning. Then, too, perhaps we were dreaming. Perhaps all we heard was an air from Shakespeare's time, pleasantly performed. All the same, for quite an interval our friend had mastered an art he knew nothing about. Right afterwards, emerging from his trance, he stared at the recorder, now silent again. Stupefied, he could not avoid recalling that it was foreign to him. He glanced at us with dread, then turned his back. As if he were lifting the curtain of the lamps, he headed off into the night, for almost an hour. As for us, we lost ourselves in conjectures—that was the evening we truly started to feel afraid.

And before long our fear turned to horror. The director had summoned us that morning, and the weather was beautiful, absolutely beautiful. As we tried to take up our work again, we spoke softly among ourselves. 'Where is Hamlet?' one of us exclaimed. Almost immediately, we heard a cry—a scream again, but this was the most frightening of all. We jumped to our feet. A hundred steps away from us, a flame rose from the ground straight to the sky, stark red and lined with a streak of black. But it had no sooner appeared than it vanished. Will you believe me? We ran over to look—and on the untouched grass, we could not help but recognize his body. Here was the actor chosen to play the role of a prince, supposedly mad. What a misfortune . . . His corpse was more than half charred but his head was intact. It lay under his right arm. He had folded that arm sharply, since he must have tried to shield himself. From what, we could not grasp. Lightning? Impossible. The sky had been blue since daybreak, intensely blue and serene.

The director closed his actor's eyes, and then we carried the body to one of our vans. We abandoned that domain of grasses and large stones where we had tried to perform Shakespeare's tragedy.

III

Today, after so many years, I am still seeking the cause, or at least the meaning, of the events that thwarted our dream of staging *Hamlet*. Those cries, those tears, that music, those flames—was it merely a long series of chance occurrences? This is what I have always wanted to believe, though I have never succeeded. And as I grow older, I have resigned myself to an explanation which—unfortunately—answers all the questions we have always asked ourselves. Somewhere outside our world, there must be a god who is displeased with his own creation. He had undertaken it with confidence and with an idea of what we can well believe was beauty—the proof of this, still today, we find in the mountains here on earth, in the rivers amid their light. But he soon perceived that the beings he was moulding did not live up to his wishes. This is only natural, since what we name a creation, at whatever level it may be, is never anything other than writing—that is, it leaves a place, possibly the main one, to the unconscious thoughts of him or her who is writing. This god had to admit to himself that there was a whole unknown and unknowable part within him, an unconscious. He had enjoyed designing the zebra's coat, with some amusement; but now he had to recognize, with a deep disquiet, that its meaning escaped him—there was a secret here, to which he would never find the key. And in the laugh of an adolescent girl, as she crossed the street with a boy, the anguish and hope that rose to the surface were equally opaque. God realized that someone within him, whom he did not know, troubled his intentions, darkened his thinking, disconcerted his intelligence. Someone? Perhaps even several wills, each contesting his power. He abandoned his unfinished schemes to the wind of that abyss.

But in his bafflement, it was only natural that he should take an interest in the theatre, where there are creatures plagued by disquiet, who imagine worlds in their own way—a new heaven, a new earth—and who feel as much as he does, in their ever-unravelling words, the disruptive force of an invisible presence. It was even more natural that he should become attached to *Hamlet*, where it is obvious that the unconscious—that great river, eternal and dark—suddenly overflows the mind from every side. In *Hamlet*, the prince does not speak; no, his voice stumbles on the obscure thoughts he harbours. He gets a grip on himself, then leaves off again—you might deduce that he has fallen prey to a constraint nothing can ever unbind. Enough to give this sad god the idea that by listening to Shakespeare's work, he might burst through whatever locked doors he hid within himself. At least he might discover whether his failure was as foreordained, for example, as the movements of the stars in their spheres—that music created for nothing.

And so God begins haunting the places where people try to understand *Hamlet*. He observes their reactions to the text and the hypotheses of actors who must reflect on their work. What emotion will he detect in Hamlet—in the actor taking the role of Hamlet—when this wholly ordinary man insults

Ophelia, when he defies Laertes, when he forces Claudius to drink the poison he feels spreading through his own veins? Won't he need to penetrate that being, or others, so he can experience what is at play—such an odd word—from within? In grasping the potential of this, in that realm of the human he had left fallow before, won't he even press it into flower as an unthinkable possibility? That is why God wants to incarnate in several of the actors in turn, even at such and such a moment of their performances, out of the depths of a particular line with which, suddenly, the actor has become as one. With sympathy, with eagerness and hope, God is ready to flood their frail bodies with the energy and fire of his infinite power. Since he has remained walled-in by that power—mysteriously flawed though it may be—it is through them that he seeks to bore his tunnel of escape.

The series of events that beset and finally ruined our rehearsals of *Hamlet* on that occasion I have evoked must reveal that he failed once again. We will never know with what a twilit anguish, with what a sadness, he must have cast his self-eviscerated gaze on life—in the distance, the clouds on fire and on the ground, the infinity of stones—when he discovered he couldn't live the emotion that blasted Ophelia; couldn't even grasp the actor's impulse, wrenched by the thought of Hecuba; or why the music born in Hamlet, just as he believes himself free of his iron-clad constraints, was but a smattering of brilliant sparks, dispelled as soon as they formed. What did he feel? That an impediment rises from the depths of matter, matter which is his essence, to snatch from his eyes what he seeks in human beings, and which even in them has never managed to bloom. That an imperious constraint, as vast as the night, sends the words back down his throat, just when he assumed he had made a simple human pain into his own. Is it absurd, my gloss on the strange events I witnessed? Of course—and first of all to my reason, on which I must rely to discredit such tall tales. But when I write—and shortly after those days in the theatre, I knew that writing was my genuine need, an irrepressible urge woven of pain and of hope—I feel very strongly that an unquiet, jealous gaze weighs me down. I experience with great clarity that someone is there, prowling along the edges of language. I even understand to perfection that the words I use desire more than what they express . . . What a sensation steals over me at times! I stand up, I look around: no one there. But all the same, I have to go out. In haste, I have to walk along the mountain path near the house where I have always lived. Here, at least, I am alone. At various distances, under the sky, huts of dry stone. Sometimes it's spring, and little flowers poke through the last patches of snow.

Walking on, I pick up one of the stones that are common in this region—grey, usually round and fairly flat, coloured here and there by tiny mosses. Stone, I look at you for quite a while. Under your lovely hues, I notice delicate, interlaced nicks that might be taken for signs. I try not to doubt what I know must be true—that these are not signs at all. And that it is better for us, stone of this world, to love you only for your gift of joining with others—which permits you for a time, now and then, to hold up an arch.

LEAVING THE GARDEN, IN THE SNOW

Another painter, one who finds it hard to understand what he should do with those last hours in the garden. The curse, the flight, the new ground, the embrace of Adam and Eve right on that ground in the night—yes, these things he grasps very well. And this is what he tries to paint.

But if he touches red, it is blood. Or black, it is a cry. If he wants to sketch a face, right away it becomes a head—and that head is immense, and stones are thrown at it from every side. If he tries to join the man and woman over there, his thought is like a giant bird that swoops down on them with beating wings and a probing beak. He wipes all this away.

I'm afraid, says Eve. Adam doesn't answer. But he takes her by the wrist and holds it tight.

On and on, the painter places steep drop-offs before them, densely thicketed, with gravel that slips from under their feet.

He forces them to keep climbing, naked though they are; he scratches their arms, flays their legs. I'm afraid, the young woman repeats. It's true that this painting continually makes a huge voice thunder against their bodies, with echoes that spill from a vast range of slopes between sky and earth.

Could this painter be God?

Wind-tossed trees . . . swollen waters the two have to cross, plunged into the torrent at one point up to their waists . . . But here's where the artist—since he is an artist, isn't he?—relents a bit, because of the body he must now give to Eve. In fact, she has just emerged from the water, dripping wet. And the water is very seductive—it slides off her shoulders in the starlight, covers her breasts, glistens faintly on her hips. With all his colour, all his draughtsmanship, the painter devotes himself to that presence. Will he clothe this young woman? Yes, a little. It's as if he were inventing beauty, before thrusting Eve and her companion even further into the night.

And so they move forward into that night, under gusts of wind that whirl without respite, though seemingly less harsh. We all know they must walk a long time, but soon the going will be easier, since they will have something like a path under their feet. Eve leads the way, even if she hesitates—everything is so dark, after all. In the nick of time, she dimly catches sight of thick branches that block their progress. The sky, still filled with stars a while ago, has retreated into its other world.

Even so, it is not cold.

And now she feels something very light on her shoulder, which the painter has left naked. A slight grazing, gently discreet. A leaf, fallen from a tree? She touches it with her finger. No, it's water.

Water, why water? But the same impalpable thing has now alighted on her neck. And soon there's another on the arm she had raised, and still another. What is this? asks Adam in turn. He has stopped. She touches his big hand, which is also somewhat wet. They start walking again.

Day breaks, little by little, and the world around them is white. It has snowed; the snow is everywhere under their feet, so each step makes a tiny sound, a kind of crunching against that sheet of white. The great snowfall covers the branches with its heft that weighs nothing.

It is as if he who was cursing them had been removed, into the sky far away, by this unknown friend. Her task achieved, now she comes to graze their bodies lightly with her fingers, which to them seem numberless.

THE DIGAMMA

In the middle of the night, he told her excitedly about the digamma: no sooner had he learnt of its existence—at thirteen, from his first professor of Greek, as the drum was already rolling for the ten o'clock recess—than he knew he was getting at the truth. In the first era of the alphabet that evolved into ours, there had been an additional letter; and the role of that letter must have been an enigma even before its disappearance. This explained everything!

Ever since that day he had dreamt a great deal, he told her. The low, maternal, slightly muffled voice, faltering at times, which accompanied him in his sorrows and his joys, had taught him more and more clearly how he should frame the great problem, perhaps the only one. Yes, she murmured, the words of those early times, letter by letter, sound by sound, matched all the aspects of things. The earth, since language was unconstrained, without a pleat of its fabric out of place along her enormous body, was as naked then as those korai would later be under their translucent tunics of bright marble. She could take us in her arms, and we dwelt within the truth. When we spoke, it was as if what we said were alive—holding us close and with its warmth on our lips. When we tried to clarify an idea, with that added rigour—yet how easy—known as poetry, it was as if we walked amid the trickling of springs and the warbling of birds, our eyes open wide.

But one day, who knows why, we began to pronounce a certain letter badly—the digamma—and because of this, the simple reality of the world was veiled. Little by little, the correspondence between words and things came to an end. The desires that united speaking beings with each other fell out of tune. There was discord in the city, which up till then had been like music. And what we have named history began, that swollen flood on an earth that it was tearing from the shore . . . Our disaster is the result of a faulty pronunciation. Can we introduce the digamma into our languages once again? Regrettably, first we would have to mend our minds, awaken our hearts.

—Our hearts?

—Maybe not . . . And you're going to tell me that if another of the letters had vanished, not the digamma, the effect on being in the world would have been pretty much the same, with a similar rupture in the harmony of speech at its source. But that isn't what I believe, my friend. Have you ever seen the digamma's shape? A lumberman's axe. It rang in the remotest forests on the mountainsides of Thrace. The old woman squatting before her fire would pick it up to chop her kindling wood. It was what broke things apart and at the same time gathered them together.

That's a lovely myth, she said. She turned towards him, in the half-light of a summer night. Through the open window near the bed, she can see the trees in the garden—two almond trees, their leaves ruffled by a faint breeze. And the blue summits of low hills, a little further away.

A myth! he exclaims. Not at all. What do you think I'm doing here? I'm studying. You know that I'm a philologist. I've read Vendryès, Dupont-Sommer—they, and all the others, attest to the existence of the digamma. I'm told that in dialects that survive on the mountains of Lucania, the digamma can still be heard. Meanwhile, all around, the timeless goats lurch down the slopes, nibbling at the leaves along the tree trunks. Sometimes the herdsmen carry a reed pipe they play, and their modest music fills the entire sky. I have a whole dossier of closely written notes; I could fill up a book with them.

Nonetheless, he explains, he won't do this, since in his arguments he always comes across a sort of knot he can't untie. As if the disappearance of the digamma had also affected logic. Still, how tempted he is to set off to those disastrously forgotten regions of Southern Italy or Central Anatolia . . .

—Among the goats, all alone? Let's go to sleep, she says. Or maybe not, since I feel as if I'm also dreaming.

She has sat up, and her voice has changed. Listen, listen! I was as beautiful then as I am today but—how can I tell you?—I was larger. Maybe I had the same eyes, but—will you understand?—they were wider open. I looked straight ahead of me. I was wearing a blue dress with a stole, of a colour that wavered between yellow and red. My sandals were so light that I went almost barefoot . . . And what was that country where I walked down the paths, for longer than I could remember? Perhaps it was the one you are telling me about . . . As it happens, I wasn't the only one who wandered like this, between earth and sky. Was he a shepherd, with his big staff in hand, the man who walked beside me? I could readily believe it, since a few steps further on we arrived at that tomb and its famous inscription. Two other young men were already there, and one of them had dropped to the ground on one knee. Leaning close, touching the stone with a finger, he was searching for a letter in one of the words.

And you as well, you who accompanied me, you lean close in turn. You want to show me that letter but you haven't recognized it there. This bewilders you very much and you look back at me when I place my hand on your shoulder. Oh yes, my friend, I see that question in your eyes and I realize you know the answer. It's not a letter that's missing in the word, it's a word that's missing in the sentence, a certain word. And this word is a verb, a verb that must be read in the present tense and—as you are well aware—in the first person. The verb that the painter, two of whose figures we are, wanted to be known as the crux of the world, but also as what always withdraws from the world.

She laughs. Her voice has already lost the solemnity that had gripped it for a moment. While speaking, she had almost sat on the edge of the bed, one leg dangling as her foot sought the coolness of the flagstones on the floor. But now she falls back again on the pillows; she stretches out and relaxes, a sensible and tender sister. Her eyes fill with the flickering reflections, coming from who knows where, on the low ceiling of the room.

And the water rises from every side. Those were not flagstones, cool or cold—this is the first flood tide of the river, broad and eternal. Do not ask me my name, she cries, already so far away. Is it a letter that is missing in the alphabet? Is it a word in language that does not exist? Isn't it simply a name, just a name that you urgently need to say? Hold on to me, hold me with all your might. Don't let go of my hand. Other forces are pulling it away. Perhaps this will be enough, even though the river is immense—roaring and dark. It overwhelms me, it carries me away. But our room is narrow—here next to us is the credenza, the mirror. All is peaceful, and sleep steals over us. That isn't the lark we hear, is it, my friend? Isn't that the nightingale?

LEARNED LIBRARIES

The library of the French School in Rome . . . Here I am, a young man doing research on the *Mirabilia Urbis Romae*, a project entrusted to me by André Chastel. And I have just made a discovery—one of those old guidebooks on a shelf, unknown to me a moment before and probably to anyone, since it's not a printed work or a manuscript, but a cup, filled with water to the brim. I pick it up with all the caution of a scribe, a philologist, and carry it to my table—which I enjoy finding free on these sultry mornings, because the window to my left overlooks the belfry of La Sapienza.

Here is the cup. I have set it down between my notebooks and my books, without spilling a drop. I examine it. Is this really water? Its coolness permeates my fingers; and what is more, it gives off reflections, which seem to disregard today's bright sun. Reflections, or, rather, images of some kind. They rise to the surface of the world and unfurl all around me, a little blurred at first and then more distinct. Where am I?

Whose hands are these I see begin to move, right before my eyes? What worries make them fidget? What are they looking for on this table stacked with things? There is a pocketknife I vaguely recognize; some books I think I read long ago; a notebook in a familiar hand, though I can't quite place it. Am I the one taking up this pen? And who in this other world has prepared me to write, yet hesitates? Who am I in fact?

But then it dawns on me—I know what chapel this is. It dates from the first Christian centuries, and its vaults enclose the monodic voice of incense. In the shadows of the side-aisles, I am working here at present. At the Clark Institute in Williamstown, Massachusetts, this is the underground library—among the few absolute places that exist on earth. And I am seated at one of the vast tables, perusing a recent book about Goya's black paintings. Now I am old. As it turned out, I never wrote my thesis on the *Mirabilia*. Nor did I often step away from some grassy street, with the evening sun at its far end, to slip into one of those small churches of Rome—the mosaics on their walls faintly glimmering, like gold within a dream. What am I doing here in the Berkshires, so late in my life? Why did I come? But of course—no doubt I am taking up again my other great project of bygone years, a study of forms and their meaning in Piero della Francesca. I used to wander with that young painter, laughing and conversing, on the gentle hills of clear Umbrian mornings. Am I going to apply myself from now on? But these are not jottings, or drafts of chapters, which my nervous hands leaf through. All they uncover beneath the notebooks and the books is a tiny mirror, beaming with light, a fire from the open sky. This astounds me, since I am two floors below ground—or so I believe.

But why should I be amazed? The mirror, its water sweet and serene, is simply the university library of Coimbra—where this time night has also fallen. Its beautiful sculpted shelves are barely visible in the faint light of low lamps. The central aisle retreats into darkness. The famous bats of this abode of poetry and learning dart silently, along a ceiling I cannot see. And there is no one seated at the tables, no one but Goya—as at the outset of the *Caprices*, racked by bad dreams, he buries his forehead in his folded arms. I stand up and sidle by him. I walk towards the end of the great room—going where, I do not know.

THE WORKS OF THE UNCONSCIOUS

In the penumbra, I discover large books, stacked on tables in a jumble. These are the works of the unconscious, I am told. In fact, the unconscious has no need of you to compose a work—how naive of you to think that only you can put him into words. Your unconscious began writing long before your birth; he paints as well, by the way. As you sleep at night, you let yourself drift through chaotic images that are but the overflow of his writing—the situations and fictions he has rejected, the scribbled sheets he scatters behind him under the great starry sky, sometimes with cries of fury because a word has escaped him. But if you paid attention, you would see him seated at his table in the dark, bent over his pen—with his tongue clamped between his teeth, he has remained such a child. And you could lean over his shoulder, look at his page and read . . .

What could I read? I open one of the volumes at random, and what I see reminds me of something, quite vaguely. All of a sudden—of course, here are two sentences I wrote years ago. I recognize them among the others, the countless others, which I draw from those folios with their big clumps of soft, rounded pages. They are drenched with water because now the rain is falling hard and a wind is blowing, a black wind. What are those other sentences next to mine? Here's one, on this paper soaked with water, which tears apart under my fingers—it's a lengthy enumeration, probably, of kings or demons or gods from eras long since forgotten. Apparently I lived in centuries I can't even imagine any more; I spoke languages that no longer exist; I was another person, or many others, unless . . .

This sentence here, this strange little girl—I've caught her by the arm and I drag her out of the book, wet as she can be. I pull her towards me, but she has no beginning and no end; by both head and toe, she plunges into constellations that are visible now all around us, even close, since the rain has stopped and the wind has cleared the sky under our feet. Yes, 'our feet', because I have multiplied. I am numerous, and we jostle in the passageways, under the vaults, with that laughter we used to hear long ago in the abyss of summer nights.

Laughter, even if I am alone after all, walking among these arcane texts that take the form of disjointed hills, strewn with flat grey stones, where here and there the summits of high columns vanish into the clouds. The unconscious has truly written a great deal. And it's a deserted country. The children who had appeared have disappeared. Their cheerful and mocking dictation is not what will enable me to recreate the world.

VOICE IN THE SOUND OF THE RAIN

I

In his room, he listens to the rain strike the tin roof on the lean-to under his window. Just beyond it stands the little peach tree, with its fruit that never ripens. A warm, summer-night rain, in large drops that sometimes fall alone or several at once, almost. And he listens to this sound, he sets himself adrift on the randomness of chance, till chance becomes his sole reality. Now he feels it well up in all things, erasing belief, figures, memories. He no longer knows who he is himself—and yet it isn't as if he has ceased to exist. Too happy for that, he has become as one with the slow plops, the brusque forward leaps of the plashing water. Child that he is, lying naked on his bed before the wide-open window, he simply lets himself go—till he is nothing more than this pounding that jumps ahead like a wild animal, this bitter smell of foliage, dark green verging on black.

But all of a sudden, what alarms him? Why does he prop himself up on one elbow, cocking his ear? Because he seems to hear a brief sequence of notes in the hammering of the drops. He'd already noticed it a few moments ago; and now—he can't tell why—it has come back once more.

And soon after that, here it is again—four or five raps on the tin, divided by an interval, the same each time. A form, in fact, a denial of the randomness I was enjoying so thoroughly, lost in its broadly gliding folds. A form? Is it possible? Has this repetition actually taken place? I listen, in the downpour that never ends, that swells instead, then slackens for a while, only to tumble down again with even greater force. I listen. Yes, right away I hear those same intervals again, without a shadow of a doubt: as if a sign were striving to free itself from happenstance. Am I dreaming? Or is it chance itself— chance, that sleep of matter—that dreams?

This form—this utterance, perhaps—recurs several times throughout the night. For long stretches I fail to hear any more; it seems to have drowned in the haphazard thrum of water on the roof. But just when I cease to believe that it was real, I perceive it once again—faintly, now and then, as if absent from itself, but this last time so loud and so close . . . No, I no longer harbour any doubts. Amid these jumbled noises of the downpour, a musician is moulding them into notes, a fragment of rhythm. A musician who loves this new-found motif. Who loves.

Maybe he even desires for someone, in our other world, to hear it too. Except that, almost in a heartbeat, the rain comes to a halt. A few lingering drops, more and more infrequent, then truly nothing at all.

II

He turns towards the woman sleeping next to him—or who seems to sleep, breathing evenly.

Did you hear? he asks her.

Yes, she says. She turns towards him; and opening her eyes, hardly visible in the dark, she stares deeply into his.

Yes, she says again. One of those prisoners.

And since she sees he is surprised: We're in prison, as you're well aware. So where is he? In one of the other cells.

Are you making fun of me?

Oh no . . .

And it's true; now he lingers over the tambourine someone—
he can't remember who—brought back to him from a coun-
try in Asia. A thin sheet of leather, stretched on a frame of
copper and wood. Despite his clumsiness, he has tapped that
surface countless times, instantly making it vibrate—with his
ear almost pressed to the rim, in hopes of recomposing that
vanished phrase. It's as if when he is writing, he aspired for
his words to retreat from their meaning, driven by a will from
underneath language itself. He listens. Is it he who plays these
notes and arranges their intervals? Or do they come from fur-
ther away—much further away—if only he could manage to
retrieve that enigmatic motif?

A hesitation on both sides. A few beats, then silence, as if
someone, somewhere, were mulling it over. And then some
taps again on the tautly stretched skin, taps that go faster at
times. Are they mine, or are they his? Who is speaking to me
there? Or to whom did I wish to speak? But all this is only a
dream—so we assume. The dream that is speech. The dream
of matter. Why should anyone be there, in the sounds of the
world? More likely, could I be the one who doesn't exist?

III

And once more this heat of a summer night and the intermittent downpour. What are you thinking about? he asks the woman who lies beside him, naked and trustful. But what answer can she give? Since the great noise of chance—that nothing, that all—has started up again, and now invades the world more and more loudly. It topples all illusions; it blankets the man and woman in its vast sheet that makes them as one. As one? More like a space without up or down, with nothing at all wandering in the void. The drops of water on the tin roof traverse it, gradually widening, until they move as far apart as the stars. And you? Do you exist, at least? he asks her, folding her in his arms. Of course, she replies, don't you hear me speaking? With his lips he seeks those lips, which are the words that will suffice.

MORE ON THE INVENTION OF DRAWING

Say what you will, drawing the shape of your lover on the wall is no easy task when he's lying on the same bed as you. Even with her chalk in hand, the young girl hates to let go of him, and still enfolds him in one of her arms. On top of that, the boy keeps moving—he bothers her, he distracts her, he makes her forget her work. And so the lamp placed behind the bed casts shadows of them both on the beautiful blank expanse—outlandish shadows that never stop shifting. In such utter disarray, try if you can to trace the curve of a shoulder on the faintly dimpled whitewash, with no more than a piece of chalk.

This explains the future history of drawing, otherwise impossible to grasp. The daughter of the Corinthian potter attempts to sketch quickly, wedding her stroke to that silhouette which means a shoulder—or a hip, for all I know. But in fact her line veers away from the contour, plunges into the shadow's heart and lingers there; it emerges only with regret, pursued by a thought that seems hard to shake off. Instead of proceeding towards the arm—this raised arm, this hand held out as if to touch the image on the nearby wall—she who merely wanted to master a line is now drawing . . . what? A sort of tree, branches that fork in all directions, numberless birds that fly through a storm-swept sky, with a gamut of feeble cries.

Her sole intent was to remember a shape. And she finds herself imagining, feeling, dreaming . . . yes, how wonderful, for a moment. The entire history of drawing, and even that of painting, will derive from this. But she has to get back to work; she's pressed for time. Soon he will be leaving, and the girl wants so much to store up her memory of him. 'Please, don't move any more!'

Come now . . . He takes the hands of this budding artist in his own, and gently pries her fingers apart. He sets the stub of chalk on the nearby table—that table where through the centuries, the lamp burns on.

Wishing to stage *Othello*, he quickly understood why his mind kept returning to those childhood evenings, when he or his loved ones had played at projecting shadows with their hands, open or closed in this way or that, on the whitewash of the roughcast wall. In fact, as the flickering flame of the candle made them quiver, the beings born of these shapes looked frightened. They seemed to shrink back from a creature that moved forward—a wolf, so we said, with a gaping maw. Were we afraid? Not too much, perhaps. But all the same, he who recalls this felt a marked unease, which pursued him to the threshold of his first dreams somewhat later in the night.

And it wasn't just that game . . . If he turned his head towards the bedroom wall before blowing out his other candle, this time he would almost undergo a wave of anguish. On the side that touched his bed, right next to him, he would see the shadow thrown by the pillow looming up—an enigmatic something, a black, fantastical mass that moved, as under the effect of a life that might have suffocated in its depths. The seething of shadows on the walls had unsettled the years of his early childhood. They made him fear that beyond the family's oil lamp and its luminous ring, lay only a mayhem of forces—destructive as well as blind. Not wanting to sleep in total darkness any more, he always kept close by him the night light's gleaming dot.

And then when he read *Othello*, his worst qualms were aroused again. *Othello* bears no resemblance to any of Shakespeare's other tragedies, even *King Lear*. In *King Lear* we cannot resign ourselves to Cordelia's death, which seems unbearable. We can understand Nahum Tate, the naive critic of the Enlightenment who rewrote the end of the drama, allowing the young woman to survive and the old king to die in peace. Indeed, it is easy to decide that those who wanted to kill Cordelia might have reached her jail after her liberators, who were already underway—by supplanting one happenstance with another, a mere stroke of the pen would free the mind from needing to think that evil could triumph so utterly. No doubt Lear had been guilty of yielding to the urges of his pride but he was not fundamentally wicked; his cries at the end of the work amply prove his capacity for love.

Othello, on the other hand . . . What facet of it could anyone think of rewriting? The perfidy of Iago unmasks this world as nothing more than an illusion. So thoroughly does it seize the Moor's mind, we find no leeway for some act of chance that might save Desdemona and restore our hope that evil is not omnipotent. Does Othello, the murderer, feel remorse? Could he begin a new life? No, he merely affirms that darkness has overwhelmed him. It hardly matters whether minor characters lead Iago off to his punishment, jeering—he has triumphed. Absolute evil, with no motivation . . . Does evil for its own sake rule the universe, the master of words that only mirror its absolute lack of meaning? Such is the question posed by this work, which goes beyond the tragic. Must we despair of the human condition?

The director takes note of what *Othello* says in this regard, or seems to say. And that is why, as he begins rehearsing the play with two actresses and several actors—women and men, in a word, who are neither better nor worse than others—he strikes upon an idea. It is vague at first, then more precise, then rapidly insistent—he won't worry about what they do with their acting on the stage; he will pay heed only to the shadows they might cast on a wall. He comes up with a contrivance. A large kerosene lamp, its flame quivering whenever a wind blows by, will be placed at the foot of the forestage where the players will perform. Their shadows will appear on a raised screen, erected at the rear of the stage; all or most of it will be visible to the audience—assuming an audience might be called for. Meanwhile the actors' voices, magnified by a loudspeaker, will bear the fateful text as they wander through gloomy space.

What justifies this shift from an actor who is very much alive—or real, so to speak—to his shade? Well, don't shadows confirm the fact of evil? For example, if we see a man or even a woman 'in shadow', most often this will mean in profile, and nothing will be left on the screen of his or her face, with all its many features, but the silhouette of the forehead, the chin, the nose. This rudimentary shape might very likely confirm what caricaturists, those cynics, are fond of suggesting—the basic animalism of human life and its unrelenting greed; the sway of matter over what appeared to be spirit. A theatre of shades would operate within the same framework as the pessimistic stance that Shakespeare's tragedy seems to expound.

Except . . . and here is the core, we might almost say the hope, of this director's thinking. Now we see him, a man still young, choose his large lamp and place it at the foot of the forestage;

we see him mark the places with some fervour, and try to enlist the actors' interest in his odd undertaking. Yes, except that these profiles, and the other bumps and hollows outlined by the shadows, say nothing, determine nothing—and this the director does not forget—about a key aspect of every human being: the features of his or her face when frontally viewed. This is when we see the look in the eyes, see the haze of the invisible that swathes the wrinkling of the brow and the movements of the mouth. The projected shadow tells us nothing of the face, nothing of what happens there, and so, doesn't that open a field for research and experimentation—leaving us room, perhaps, for some kind of future? And by not showing the face, doesn't the shadow reveal its otherness? Could we even say, and could we hope, that it protects our chance to escape from our imprisonment in matter? The shadow has not succeeded in compromising this. No more than the squalid smiles of certain old men, in the *Caprices*, sully the faces of young girls whom Goya sketches at other moments—and at another level of himself. The shadow, the projected shadow, only drains the silt from the bed of the river. Nonetheless, for as long as *Othello* continues to be staged, perhaps the work's strange text in poetry and prose—delivered just as it is and with no other support but itself—will let us sense more clearly, in its difficult depths, a possibility that is smothered in its everyday performances.

The willow song would be thrown into such deep relief, with Desdemona reduced to the shadow of a seated woman—her semi-nude body traced on the screen with a certain graceful-ness, all the same . . . It would be the voice, the true place of poetry, which would prevail over all the other forms that man-ifest what we call reality. We would think of the accord—promising, perhaps—between music and words. We would no longer perceive this as an enigma but as a sign. We would remember that the hapless Ophelia as well, in her troubled final moments, repaired to a willow to weave garlands—pen-sively, as Shakespeare writes. A tree, one of the lovely, simple features of our earthly surroundings, would loom in the spec-tator's mind with its endless branches and leaves, untroubled by any interpretation of its salutary presence.

The actor the director had chosen for Othello was a genial fellow who seemed devoid of malice. He had suffered to see the man insult Desdemona, shouting out those dreadful words—after all, his gaze was so beautiful at times, almost that of a child. How could he let such a mystery succumb, helplessly, to the traitor's devastating logic?

And so he set to work. The lamp burnt high and bright. As required by each scene, he placed the actors before it in groups of two or more. He watched their shadows moving in its beam; and as it turned out, on the screen their gestures assumed an unexpected heft. No more faces, of course; instead there were heads that fused together and scarily freakish hair. In addition there were arms that jutted out of bodies: they jumped forward and seemed to waver with open hands, then retreated into a character's shadow—at times that of an actor who had no lines. On the white canvas, always shuddering a little, even supernumeraries in small roles deployed a mass of opaqueness they would never have had on stage, and which looked quite disturbing. Then there were moments when two shadows mingled, locked in a kind of tussle—or so it seemed—which could not have been foreseen . . . Night was certainly at work in these sudden bursts, these intertwining shades. But did she alone act upon reality, now that this experiment had begun? Thereby authorized to exist on her own, was she sidetracked from an intuition that might raise its voice entirely elsewhere?

Lamentably, this experimenter with shadow theatre must clearly note that he has failed to give free rein to the evil he wishes to fight; in other words, to remove from its claws that human face which he dreams is of a wholly different nature. Since where the face has vanished, the gesture has come to the fore. There are gestures on the glowing screen, in these rehearsals of *Othello*, which show nothing more than dreary black profiles of a fidgeting, primal life: insects twitching their mandibles or jaws clamping on their prey. But there are also those that display—merely for a second, to be sure—a certain grace; or better yet, a kind of hesitancy that seems to recall, encircled as these gestures are by night, an appeal they have heard. This is especially true towards the end of the play, when Emilia and Desdemona speak to each other as two women, and later do so again. A movement, a hand that ventures towards another, a way of standing up and walking— all are stitched on the white background by a plethora of light. The shining lamp effaces neither the fright that grips Desdemona nor the hope she cannot renounce; both remain in the shadows of her gestures. This spells ruin for the director's endeavour, since those gestures have become a face once again. He cannot help but grasp his fiasco: his inability to divide the transcendence of which he dreams from that sad reality his shadow theatre was meant to display.

What should he do? Naturally enough, the director then resolved to dispense with the actors, those irreducible bearers of their own ambiguity. Instead, he would accompany the text of *Othello* with another family of projected shadows—those cast by mere imitations of life. They would not even be the works of artists; just the mannequins that vendors of artists' materials offer for sale to draughtsmen who have no models. Four limbs made of wood mounted on ball joints. Egg-shaped heads unmarked by any features. These minimal forms could mime the situations in the play. Stagehands sitting near the dummies would lift them and make them move without concealing their own presence, since at ground level their shadows would only add more disquiet to the unease instilled by *Othello*. And the creaking effigies would render the action jerky, with their stops and starts. But owing to this, wouldn't time itself, time as such, confess that it too is no more than matter, bereft of any meaning? Even though it lies at the heart of undertakings and events we would deem uniquely human, and permeates our most intimate encounters.

The director bought the mannequins—there are life-size dummies sold commercially, who knows why. He arranged them in front of his trusty lamp, though this was no easy task: they didn't stand up well and they knocked each other over. Even so, at times they stayed upright for a moment, when they found support on each other's limbs.

But he couldn't have felt more astonished. Was he only dreaming from now on, in his anxiety to set in motion these large, inert objects? In any case, he was far from breaking—breaking at last, as he had wished—with every vain trace of ordinary hope. Though he manipulated the shadows of a good many dummies, it appeared to him that all they ever conveyed was that hope. Beneath the strange life of the signs they seemed to draw and offer him on the screen, that blank page, that empty whiteness was making a mysterious proposal, at once inviting and sealed off. Undoubtedly, these were shadows of a different sort from before. Yes, they were abstract, tangled, baffling and muddled; but surprisingly, they resembled a form of writing.

Stirred to his inmost depths, the director had an inkling that letters, if not words, unknown to him and to everyone—in this space between the present and God knows what future—were trying to forge a shape, to take on meaning. Perhaps a writing, a language with vital words, would answer the offer extended by the whiteness, would already speak with it then. The world's basic matter was always there, in the bumps and the hollows. But even at their most dreadful, they were steeped in this new genre of activity, which seemed to cast shadows only when it could warrant they would stand out at the insistence of a light. Nevertheless, the thought that appeared to issue from *Othello*—the observation by Iago and his ilk that life multiplies without end—gave up this struggle of sign and darkness for lost. From the first day, the adoption of a shadow theatre had aimed to avoid that collision; if it possessed any faith at all, it was in a grace from beyond this base world.

Certainly, it was hard to assent to such a risk; and so, before long, the director of this troupe of rebellious shadows found himself on quite a different path. What did he want, what did he do? He piled his mannequins into a van and went off at night to look for fields dotted with tall stones. Among them he picked out a setting, and this time he raised the old screen under the moon, between earth and sky. Then he lit his lamp amid the boulders; its flame never varied, as if heedless of his enterprise. In front of it, he unloaded those jumbled limbs of the dead; and though he propped them up, they tottered as before. And it was there, of course, by projecting the hybrid shadows of dummies and rocks—nothing but the random, senseless scree of our vacuous world—that he hoped to wipe all memory of the face from his screen at last, and let the kind of truth that denies it live on in the dregs of non-being. Meanwhile, the text of *Othello* would go on seeking its way, thanks to a gramophone placed in the grass.

Do we need to tell the rest? The human element would not vanish, even from the most bizarre and frightening shadows the director put to the test among these piles of stone. There were always moments when in their sheer, meaningless brutality, he was forced to recognize . . . What? I would say it was the bowed head of Desdemona, pensive and infinitely sad, still otherworldly and full of hope. Abandoned by his stagehands from now on, he was alone as he packed his mannequins into the van. The day had begun to dawn, already washing the shadows from his screen. Soon he would simply have to understand what he had not known, or had not wanted to know: in order to be ourselves, and to accede to the greater meaning, we must never deprive the human face of its flesh; and the world of matter itself—however disastrous it may be—is where the absolute, that tiny flower, must bloom.

THE GREAT VOICE

I was in the land of Shakespeare, staying at the house of a friend—a professor, a poet. On Sunday morning, I found out he would be attending a church service, as he did each week, and I told him—without really thinking so—that I would enjoy going with him. The stark modesty of the chapel of grey stone seemed well suited to preserving a faith that is now rather shaky, perhaps; to an unbeliever, its plainness was appealing as well. We seated ourselves in the large room; it was still almost empty, though it quickly filled up behind us. These new arrivals inhabited the few houses nearby, a village not far from the university where my friend was teaching. Presently the celebrant appeared, and gave a sermon I considered tedious. In the meantime, my eyes wandered over the sculptures on the walls and on the capitals, as a ray of winter sun slowly inched along them. At a certain point, the pastor stopped speaking and the congregation began to sing. A simple tune carried by naive voices, exactly as intended by the black, dog-eared books I had noticed, scattered along the pews, when we had chosen our seats. A music to make us consent to the insignificance of our lives—possibly with a remnant of expectation, or of childhood, in the unison that it required.

The singing had already lasted a minute or two when out of the blue, an unheralded voice arose—it soared gloriously through the light and shade of the chapel, taking possession of the hymn. A woman's voice, young and profound. A contralto voice, but of a range that surpassed its tessitura, and with surges in volume that never distorted its timbre in the least—on the contrary, they deepened it, embellished it, transfigured it. Might I even dare to say they rendered it more human? Though isn't it true that the human, in ordinary circumstances, always falls short of its huge potential? The voice moved through the hymn with perfect ease, at once relaxed and intensely serious. It lifted the singing of the others on its wings with a gracious welcome, as well as with indifference, since it was entirely at the summit of itself, in that sphere of the spirit where the essence of the feminine could flower at long last . . . Was I dreaming? Yes, no doubt; I made an effort to wake up and I succeeded, more or less. All the same, the voice there behind me, gliding above everything, was unusual and disconcerting. Once the observance came to an end, we rose from our seats amid the hubbub of footsteps and pews. People were already leaving the room when I saw a young woman cross the porch, pushing the wheelchair of an invalid.

'Who on earth are they?' I asked my friend, and he explained that the woman walking away from us and the man she helped to go on living were husband and wife. Though not so old, he had fallen victim to a sudden illness. She was a singer; to take care of him, she had abandoned a career that promised to be as exceptional as her voice—her great voice. The two of them kept to themselves, in a cottage set apart somewhat from the village; it may have been the childhood home of one of them. The only visitor they received was the doctor, people said. Of course, she didn't sing any more, except at the Sunday service. That was all my friend knew. While he spoke, I watched the singer and the invalid, fairly far away from us by now—haltingly, they followed a path that climbed a bit. At times, to negotiate an uneven patch of ground, she had to shove the back of the wheelchair with both hands.

Several years have gone by since that morning, but I have never forgotten that hymn, that voice and that young woman returning with her stricken husband—in silence, most likely—to their secluded house. There she grows old, and her voice might be declining. I tell myself that life has treated her unfairly; I feel the wrong she has suffered should be set right somehow, at least in part. And could I do something to that end? Her voice sang for no one in a church; could I help make it known at any rate, if not heard, as a kind of testimonial? But how should I go about it? Writing is what I know how to do; my only resource is telling tales, and all in vain . . . When we write we stay locked inside ourselves, prey to the past that is ours and to desires we cannot fathom. We have no inkling of others, except for the signs they may lend to this shadow of speech; we do not give, we take. Through words, I have tried in various ways to grant life to a remembrance that has never ceased to haunt me, but I have always done so by imagining, more or less, by devoting myself to fiction. And yet, as I could not forget, the singer had withdrawn from such a life; by being heard and acclaimed, she would have become a fiction for others, and probably for herself.

And I can say, as I do at present, that I reject such literature; however, even as I write that, I am still the one who is expressing himself. All the same, a thought has come to me; that is why today I have decided to evoke that morning from the past. A thought—the imagination once again but with something added: that it will not mask the contradiction I have just pointed out. There may have been—'once upon a time', as tales used to put it—a young man. Very young, let's say. That winter morning, he entered the chapel through its low-ceilinged porch and found himself caught up in an observance. Behind him he heard that voice, both imaginary and real—redolent, to phrase it differently, of more than this base, always self-centred realm of words. But unlike me, he would have lingered in the village; he would even have lived there for days, going to loiter at times near the silent thatched cottage. In front of it were clear hints of an ordinary existence: a car, two steps away; sometimes a basket on the threshold, with things inside; even a watering can, since small flowers had already sprung up along the wall; and also—so he notices—a plume of smoke above the chimney built of bricks.

A life. But the door and the windows are closed. Without a trill to break the silence unexpectedly, only to leave it stranger than before. The young man—but he may be an adolescent, or even a child, abashed as we are at that age by any kind of sheer amazement—clearly would not dare to knock at this front door that so enthralls him. Still, he constantly returns to the edge of the garden in front of the house. He even ventures into it one day, approaching the threshold, closer and closer.

And suddenly, he doesn't know how, here is the singer right before him, just a few paces away; watering can in hand, she looks at him in astonishment. Up till now, he's only seen her from afar, with her back to him. Whom does she resemble? That is his question, right away. Is she beautiful? He couldn't say. What strikes him about these eyes that fix their gaze on him, these eyes of a faded blue, is that he has surely seen them before, and that they recognize him, too—something in his entire body tells him so. She looks at him. 'Who are you?' she asks. She may have felt a tremor of fear but she has quickly recovered.

He doesn't know what to reply—those eyes, and their light, are dissolving the garden and the house; dissolving the figure who stands before him, in her quaint dress from another age, and even the face itself. 'Who are you?' Yes, who is he? And does he even exist? It's all too much for him. This is what takes hold of his inmost mind, his inmost anxiety, and expands them, flattens them, disperses them in the growing light. 'Who am I?' He knows very well he couldn't answer. It's as if he were waking up, as if his own eyes were flooded by dawn.

What is a voice when it has turned into song? When it rises above the others without consigning them to ordinary music, no matter how naive and humble they may be? What is a fiction that seeks to mesh with the immaterial curves of this balcony between earth and sky?

THE DIGAMMA: A FINAL NOTE

The digamma's disappearance from the alphabet of the Greek language was probably not what one of my characters imagines—the cause of a later disjunction between things and the intellect in the societies of the Western world. But when he learnt that the letter had vanished, adolescent that he was, it may well have caught his attention, since it leads us to think of other eclipses—for example, that of our knowledge of finitude, within the networks of conceptual meanings. A kind of defective pleat then arises between existence and its verbal clothing, a fold beneath speech that never stops shifting, without being reabsorbed into words. Owing to this, words will always be a fiction, despite the efforts—though in fact they are dreams—of what our own era has designated as writing: which bears witness, after all, to our need for poetry.